The Mysteries of Abu Simbel

The Mysteries of Abu Simbel

Ramesses II and the Temples of the Rising Sun

To Laura

Zahi Hawass

Foreword by
H.E. Farouk Hosni
Minister of Culture

The American University in Cairo
Cairo • New York

Frontispiece: Nineteenth-century drawing of the entrance to the Great Temple of Abu Simbel.

The American University in Cairo Press
113 Sharia Kasr el Aini, Cairo, Egypt
420 Fifth Avenue, New York, NY 10018
http://www.aucpress.com

Dar el Kutub No. 17313/00
ISBN 977 424 623 3

Printed in Egypt

Foreword

King Seti I, a king of Dynasty 19, said to his son Ramesses II, "Rule with your father in your youth, and your age will extend forever." This was the prophecy of the genius pharaohs who founded their kingdoms on both strength and science. At a time when other civilizations of the world were still in their early childhood, the Egyptian dynasties were at the peak of their greatness.

Ramesses ruled for a long time and established a great kingdom, spreading Egypt's glory from the east to the west with wondrous achievements. For example, his temple at Abu Simbel, that great gateway to the south, set fear in the hearts of his enemies before they even set foot in the land of Egypt.

The temple was a marvelous achievement, uniting both genius art and great architecture, to the extent that we find not a single mistake in its construction. To console him in his solitude in the afterlife, he built for his beloved wife Nefertari a temple that imbued the site with magic and mystery that attest to the achievements of the great pharaohs.

Could Ramesses have ever imagined for a moment that his descendents so many hundreds of years later would cooperate with the modern world to perpetuate his name? And now, its glory shines while its stones have been made to speak through the Sound and Light show that tells the story of this majestic and glorious history.

Farouk Hosni
Minister of Culture

Introduction

In November 1974, Dr. Hassan Sobhi el-Bakri, then head of the Inspectorate and Excavations Division of the Egyptian Antiquities Organization, asked me to serve as Inspector of Antiquities at Abu Simbel for three months. I took the job in December, staying through February of 1975. As inspector, I was in charge not only of the monuments, but also of the settlement that was built in 1960 to house the archaeologists, engineers, and administrators of the salvage campaign.

I spent a wonderful three months at the site, studying the architecture of the two beautiful rock-cut temples and examining the scenes that cover their walls, even solving some of the puzzles presented by the decoration. I enjoyed meeting the people who came to see the sights and eat the fresh fish that was caught in the lake in front of the temple. At sunset, I would bask in the desert silence that blanketed the site after the daily airplane had come and gone; the only people remaining on the site with me in the evening were the doctor of the clinic, the chief of police, and the tour guide.

Since 1974, Abu Simbel, which is part of the Aswan governorate, has grown into a large city headed by a mayor. It now has two hotels, and three to four thousand tourists visit the temples every day. The area is thriving, and the silence has been replaced by the excitement of a vibrant city.

The Pyramids of Meroe.

I feel privileged that Mr. Farouk Hosni, Minister of Culture, has asked me to write this book to be used as a guide for both Egyptians and foreigners who visit the site of Abu Simbel. At his suggestion, there will also be a large-format book so that photographs of this beautiful site will be available to those interested in the temples of Ramesses II and his queen, Nefertari. Minister Hosni has suggested that the American University in Cairo Press cooperate with a worldwide publisher to print the latter book, and Mr. Mark Linz, head of the AUC Press, has welcomed the idea. This book is the first part of this project.

The new sound and light show at Abu Simbel is beautifully done, and includes projections of many of the interior scenes of the temples. Tourists can clearly see them in this way without entering the temple and damaging these irreplaceable reliefs.

I would like to thank my dear friend, the late Dr. Gamal Mokhtar, for providing me with information about the salvaging of the two temples. I would also like to thank my colleague, Dr. Janice Kamrin, for editing the English version of this book, and my friend Ken Garret for providing this book with some photos. I am also, of course, grateful to Mark Linz and the AUC Press for publishing this book.

Zahi Hawass

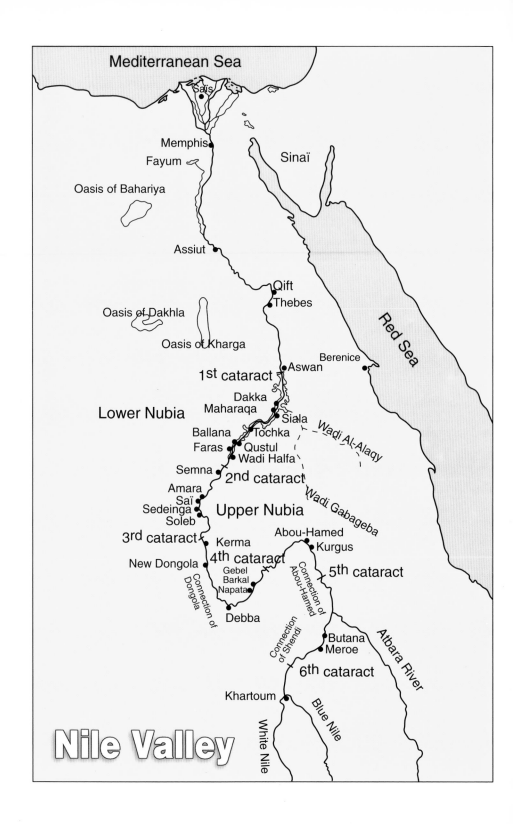

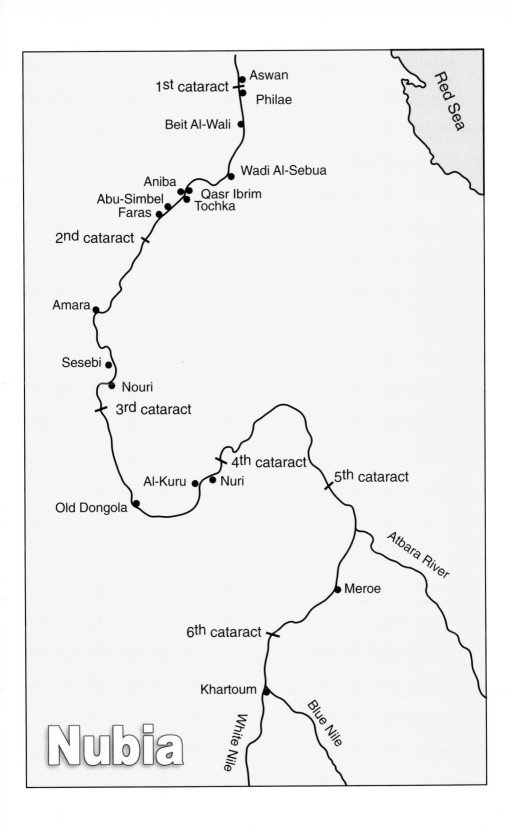

1st cataract

Aswan

Philae

Beit Al-Wali

Wadi Al-Sebua

Aniba

Abu-Simbel

Faras

Qasr Ibrim

Tochka

2nd cataract

Amara

Sesebi

Nouri

3rd cataract

4th cataract

Al-Kuru

Nuri

5th cataract

Old Dongola

Atbara River

Meroe

6th cataract

Khartoum

White Nile

Blue Nile

Red Sea

Nubia

*The colossal statue
of Ramesses II
at the new Nubian
Museum - Aswan.*

Nubia

The temples of Abu Simbel lie about 280 km (170 miles) south of Aswan, in a region known to the ancients as Nubia. This geographical term first appears in about 25 BC in the writings of the Greek historian and geographer Strabo, who used it to refer to the area of African desert bisected by the Nile that extends from the First Cataract at Aswan in the north to the Fourth Cataract in the south. The area was traditionally divided into two distinct geographical regions, each with its own unique climate and topography. Lower Nubia, now largely under Egyptian control, includes the area between the First and Second cataracts, while Upper Nubia, which belongs to Sudan, extends from the Second Cataract to the Fourth Cataract.

By 3050 BC, Egyptian expeditions had traveled south at least as far as the Second Cataract. At this time, the deserts flanking the Nile were wetter than they are now, and significantly large populations occupied both Upper and Lower Nubia. By 2500, at the height of the Egyptian Old Kingdom, the Sahara had dried up, and Lower Nubia was occupied only by sparse nomadic bands. Upper Nubia, which had a larger amount of fertile soil, continued to develop its own distinctive and highly evolved civilization.

From earliest times, Nubia was a bridge between the southern civilizations in the heart of Africa and the Egyptian and Mediterranean cultures to the north. As a consequence, Nubian culture was a hybrid of the southern African cultures on the one side and the cultures of Egypt, Greece, and Rome on the other. However, the strongest influence came from Egypt because of its close proximity, the similarity of its topography, and the military and political contacts that were established at least as early as the third millennium BC.

The waxing and waning of Egypt's strength can be traced through its relations with Nubia. When strong kings ruled a united land, Egyptian influence extended into Nubia; when Egypt was weak, its southern border stopped at Aswan.

Nubia was a very important source of trade goods such as ivory, wood, leather, incense, and exotic animals such as monkeys and giraffes. Gold, granite, and diorite were also mined in Nubian quarries. In fact, gold was so plentiful in Nubia that the name comes from the word for gold in ancient Egyptian. The importance of gold to the Egyptians is underlined in a letter from the king of the Mittani to King Amenhotep III, which says, "send me gold in your country ... gold is like dust."

During the Old Kingdom, Egypt traded peacefully with the inhabitants of Upper Nubia, which they called Yam. In order to protect their trade routes from the nomadic bands who lived in Wawat, or Lower Nubia, the Egyptians established a series of settlements in the area. These were abandoned in about 2420 BC, when the centralized Egyptian government lost power and the country splintered into the competing dynasties of the First Intermediate Period.

By the Middle Kingdom, Upper Nubia was ruled by the powerful kingdom of Kush, which represented a military threat to Egypt. The kings of the Twelfth Dynasty responded by building a series of impressive fortresses that secured the region from the First to the Second Cataract. Kush and Egypt continued to trade, but in an atmosphere more of armed truce, with Egypt maintaining Lower Nubia as a buffer zone. Campaigns were frequently mounted into the area to subdue rebellious natives and to control the flow of trade from the south, and the Egyptians did their best to Egyptianize the Lower Nubians and enforce their loyalty to Egypt.

In about 1650 BC, as Egypt once again fell into internal disarray, the rulers of Kush invaded Lower Nubia and took over the Egyptian forts. During the Second Intermediate Period, the Egyptians also lost control of the north of their own country to the Hyksos, foreigners from the northeast who ruled from Avaris (near to the future site of Per Ramesses) in the Delta.

In one of the lowest points of pharaonic history, the Hyksos in the north and the Kushites in the south formed an alliance against the native Egyptians who were ruling their remaining territory from Thebes. Apophis, the Hyksos king, sent a messenger to the ruler of Kush inviting him to join forces and attack the Egyptian king. Fortunately, the messenger was caught by the Egyptians at the border of the Bahriya oasis, and disaster was averted.

After the Egyptians expelled the Hyksos from Egypt, they made good use of the lessons they had learned. Between about 1570 and 1500 BC, the Egyptians reestablished control over the Lower Nubian fortresses and extended their empire into Upper Nubia, all the way to Napata, just north of the Fourth Cataract. Until the end of the New Kingdom, ca. 1085 BC, both Lower and Upper Nubia were colonial possessions of Egypt. The native rulers were replaced with Egyptian or Egyptianized governors who answered to the Egyptian king at Thebes. Nubian soldiers and bowmen from the Eastern Desert served in the Egyptian army, and even fought with the Egyptian kings on campaigns into Syria and Palestine. There were occasional rebellions, but these seem to have been put down quickly, and Egyptian control over the area was maintained.

*Ramesses II, The Pharaoh
of Eternity - Abu Simbel .*

Nineteenth-century drawing of the Great Temple of Abu Simbel.

A number of New Kingdom pharaohs built chapels and temples in Nubia, establishing them as religious centers where Egyptian gods and kings were worshiped. These temples played an important role in Egyptianizing the people of Nubia, and guaranteeing their loyalty to the pharaoh as the embodiment of god on earth. The temples of Ramesses II at Abu Simbel represent the most magnificent of these Nubian temples, a living testament to the power and wealth of the Egyptian empire.

After the fall of the Egyptian New Kingdom, native rulers reasserted control over Nubia. In fact, the kings of the Napatan culture, centered around the Fourth Cataract, grew so strong that they invaded Egypt and ruled it for a short time (ca. 751–656 BC) as the Twenty-fifth Dynasty. Christianity entered Nubia from the north and reigned supreme until Islam was introduced and rapidly became the dominant religion. It is fascinating to note that Nubian Muslims are among the most devoted practitioners of Islam in the world today.

Ancient Nubia became known to Western civilization during the nineteenth century. The first important western visitor to Nubia was John Lewis Burckhardt, who went by camel from Aswan to Dongola in 1813. Many others followed in his footsteps: Jean Nicolas Huyot, François-Chrêtien Gau, Karl Richard Lepsius, James Breasted, and Wallis Budge, among others. Each of these published valuable descriptions of the monuments they saw during their journeys through Nubia and Egypt.

Abu Simbel was first noted in 1813 by Burckhardt, who suspected that a vast temple lay beneath the desert sands. The first European to clear sand from the temples at Abu Simbel was circus strongman Giovanni Belzoni, who uncovered the entrance to the Great Temple in 1817.

In 1907, George Reisner started the first important scientific survey and excavation of Nubia. This survey was continued by C. M. Firth from 1908 to 1911, and resulted in fifteen illustrated volumes on the Nubian temples and a detailed description of the monuments and cemeteries in the area. Many other survey and excavation projects were carried out in the area until 1959, when it was announced that a high dam would be built at Aswan.

Avenue of sphinxes of the Temple of Ramesses II at el-Sebua.

Nineteenth-century drawing of Abu Simbel.

The High Dam

The monuments of Nubia were protected for thousands of years by the sand that buried them and shielded them from the ravages of wind and time. Their remote locations kept them from being destroyed by the spread of modern civilization, although many of these temples were converted to churches after the introduction of Christianity.

The temples and churches of Lower Nubia were first threatened in 1902, when the Egyptian government built a dam at Aswan that created a reservoir of water to the south. This dam was rebuilt in 1912 and 1936, in both cases resulting in further water damage to monuments within the reach of the rising reservoir waters. At that time, the Egyptian Antiquities Organization began restoration and conservation projects to confront this threat.

In the 1950s, the Egyptian government decided to replace the current small dam at Aswan with a much larger dam. This was to be constructed of rock, and was to measure 3,600 m (12,000 ft) long, 40 m (130 ft) wide, 180 m (600 ft) at its base, and rise to a height of 104 m (340 ft) above sea level. Floods to a height of 182 m (597 ft) can be held back by the dam. The artificial lake created by the dam, Lake Nasser, extends 500 km (315 miles) in length, stretching south beyond the Second Cataract, and up to 25 km (16 miles) in width.

The Aswan High Dam was begun in 1960 and finished in 1964, and represents one of Egypt's most successful national projects since the age of the pyramids. It is the soul of modern Egypt, and represents the power, strength, and dignity of the modern state. By means of this dam, the waters that once flooded the land every year can be controlled and used efficiently. No longer a victim of the irregular and unpredictable floods that produced the years of feast and famine that are woven into the fabric of Egyptian history, Egypt now enjoys control over its own fate. The High Dam also provides Egypt with electrical power for the villages that line the Nile, thereby helping to raise the cultural and educational level of the entire country.

There has been a great deal of concern in the world media about the effect of the High Dam on the monuments of Egypt. The salinity of the water table that underlies the bedrock of the Nile Valley has risen dramatically over the course of the past fifty years, causing salt to leach into the walls of the ancient monuments and eat away at their surfaces. It was long believed that the High Dam was causing this terrible problem; however, recent scientific analysis has shown that the deterioration of the monuments can be traced to salt-filled runoff from the many villages that still lack modern sewer systems.

One of the heads of Ramesses II - Abu Simbel.

The UNESCO Salvage Campaign

Despite the many potential benefits of the High Dam, Egypt faced the huge problem of saving the archaeological sites that would disappear under the waters of the expanded reservoir. These monuments included not only major temples such as those Abu Simbel, but also chapels and settlement remains, stelae, inscriptions, and as yet undiscovered sites. The Egyptian government recognized that in order to be effective and timely, a salvage campaign to rescue the monuments needed international support, and sought the help of UNESCO.

This was the first such request UNESCO had received since its inception in 1954. The Executive Council welcomed the request of the Egyptian government when it met in July of 1959. The council agreed that the monuments of Lower Nubia represented a unique part of the ancient heritage of humankind. The extreme antiquity of the sites and their location in an isolated and sparsely inhabited area of the world made them a perfect focus for an international relief effort.

On March 8, 1960, a historic event, attended by many important international figures, took place in Paris. Vittorino Veronese, the General Secretary of UNESCO from 1958 to 1961, and his successor, Rene Maheu, president of UNESCO from 1961 to 1974, called on governments, international organizations, and any group concerned with our international heritage to provide help in the form of funds or technical assistance. The response was overwhelming: committees and researchers from over twenty countries worked together for twenty years on the highly successful campaign launched by this event.

A thorough record of the monuments of Lower Nubia was made in a very short period of time and many salvage excavations were carried out. The single most impressive accomplishment of the committee was the moving of the Abu Simbel temples from their location directly in the path of Lake Nasser to a higher location out of reach of the water. Many countries, including the United States, France, and Germany, and individuals such as Madame Lila-Atcheson Wallace, owner of *Reader's Digest* maga-

Preparing the statues of Ramesses II of the Great Temple to be moved.

zine, contributed generously in both time and money toward this operation, which took five years and cost forty-two million dollars. The most
remarkable contribution came from children all over the world, who sent
their allowance money to help with the salvage effort. The world media
gave the campaign enormous attention and support, and UNESCO sent
out scholars to lecture on the importance of the campaign. Films, books,
posters, and photographs about the temples were widely published.

The successful Nubian campaign prompted other countries to petition
UNESCO to help save their own monuments. Campaigns were mounted
to help preserve the canal city of Venice in Italy, the Acropolis of Athens
in Greece, the ancient city of Mohenjodaro in Pakistan, Barabudur in
Indonesia, and Fez in Morocco.

UNESCO and Egypt did a marvelous job of acquainting the world with
the problem of the Nubian monuments and of inspiring people of all ages
and categories to help. Men, women, and children all responded with
enthusiasm and support, and their combined contributions helped to save
the beautiful temples of Abu Simbel for posterity. The most spectacular of
the threatened Nubian monuments were the two temples at Abu Simbel,
which lay directly in the path of the new reservoir.

The original site of the two temples of Abu Simbel .

Salvaging the Abu Simbel Temples

These temples had been carved into the living rocks of a cliff overlooking the Nile by Ramesses the Great. The larger of the two temples was dedicated to Ramesses II himself and the gods Re-Horakhti, Amen-Re, and Ptah. The smaller temple was built for Ramesses' principal queen, Nefertari, and the goddess Hathor.

In 1959, a committee of experts and consultants was established specifically to focus on saving the rock-cut temples at Abu Simbel. This committee included both Egyptian and international experts in architecture, engineering, archaeology, planning, and finance; they worked from 1959 until 1963 to save the temples from the waters of Lake Nasser.

The first and most crucial task facing the experts was to evaluate the various proposals that were brought to them. One proposal suggested leaving the temples in place and building concrete tubes around them as protection from the encroaching waters. The temples would then have become marine museums, reachable by elevator.

Another proposal, made by a team of French engineers, suggested cutting the two temples from their rock setting, surrounding them with a protective covering, and placing them on two plateaus that would rise with the rising waters of the lake, and then moving them to shore in a new location.

A third proposal suggested that a half circle of concrete be built at a distance of 300 m (984 ft) from the monuments. The height and location of the new dam would have allowed the rays of sun to continue to enter the temples and illuminate the inner sanctuaries. This proposal would have preserved the beauty of the original magnificent setting of the temples. However, the temples would have been in a hollow entirely surrounded by water that reached 60 m (almost 200 ft) above the temples. The porous sandstone of the temples could have easily been penetrated by any overflow, causing irreparable damage to the monuments. A giant pumping station was also proposed to obviate this problem, but if anything went wrong with the station, the monuments could have been destroyed forever.

Lifting one of the Ramesses heads.

The cost of this proposal was also enormous, over 80 million dollars, and was rejected by both Egypt and UNESCO.

Another proposal was submitted by Professor Piero Gozzola, a professor of civil engineering at the University of Milan. He suggested removing the temples from the mountain in which they had been built, surrounding them with protective covering, moving them to a height of 65 m (213 ft), and setting them down in a new location while preserving their original orientation. Under this proposal, the mass of rock above the temples would also be moved to the new location (but separately, to facilitate the moving of the temples themselves), and the original environment surrounding the temples would be recreated as accurately as possible.

This last proposal was accepted by the Egyptian government on July 20, 1961, but with a great deal of reservation, since it called for almost 350,000 tons to be lifted to a height of 65 m. The only previous experience in this area had been the moving of a church weighing less than 10,000 tons to a height of a mere 2 m (about 6.5 ft).

It was finally decided to implement a slightly different proposal, which called for the temples to be cut into large blocks and reassembled in a new location. The original orientation would be carefully maintained, and an artificial mountain would be built around them to recreate their original settings. The principal advantage of this proposal was that it was significantly safer and less costly, but some archaeologists objected vehemently, describing the cutting of the stones and statues as the butchering of the Abu Simbel temples. Fortunately, history proved them wrong, and the moving of the Abu Simbel temples was carried out safely and successfully, a jewel in the crown of the Nubian salvage campaign.

The salvaging of the Abu Simbel temples was carried out in seven stages:

(1) A temporary dam was built in front of the two temples to protect them from the rising water. This dam was 730 m (2,400 ft) long and 37 m (121 ft) high, and was built from 38,000 cubic m (1.3 million cubic ft) of sandstone. The front of the Great Temple was covered with sand to protect the giant statues from the pressure that resulted when the walls behind them were covered with scaffolding to prepare them for removal.

(2) More than 150,000 cubic m (5 million cubic ft) of rock was moved from the two cliffs above the temples.

(3) The stones, statues, and columns of the temples were cut into giant pieces ranging from 3 to 20 tons in weight, each with a height of 3 m and a length of 5 m (approximately 10 ft by 16 ft). The Great Temple was cut into 807 pieces, while the Temple of Nefertari was cut into 225 blocks.

(4) After the new site was prepared, the large blocks from the temple were lifted to the new chosen site.

(5) The two temples were rebuilt on their new site, with the original orientations reproduced carefully. The most moving moment of this operation

was in March of 1967, when the crowns of Ramesses II were placed atop the giant statues in front of the temple. This was a great moment that no one involved in the project will ever forget: the most advanced technology of the twentieth century was used to save one of the most amazing achievements of a civilization that preceded it by 3,300 years.

(6) Two concrete domes were built above the temples to protect them from the weight of the rocks that were piled above them. The domes above the Great Temple is one of the largest artificial dome in the world, with a circumference of 60 m (nearly 200 ft) and a height of 22 m (84 ft).

(7) Artificial hillocks were built above the two temples to recreate their original setting. These hillocks used a total of 230,000 cubic m (more than 8 million cubic ft) of sandstone.

This enormous endeavor, unparalleled in history, was carried out by a consortium of the following companies: the French company Grands Travaux de Marseilles, Hoch-Tief of Germany, Impregito of Italy, two Swedish companies, Sentabex and Shanska, and the Egyptian company Atlas. All of the work was supervised by the Swedish group VBB.

Before work was started, a modern city was built to accommodate the more than 3,000 Egyptian and foreign workers, many accompanied by their families, who carried out the project. Despite the remote location of the site, the difficulties of transport and communication, and the harsh weather (the temperature in the summer can reach 50°C/122°F in the shade), great care was taken to house the workers in the most modern and comfortable facilities possible.

Preparing one of the Ramesses heads to be constructed on the new site.

The removal of one of the Ramesses heads.

The project cost 42 million dollars and was concluded in under five years. It began in November of 1963 and finished in September 1968, twenty months before the originally estimated end date. No stone was lost or damaged, no changes in design were made, and the temples appear exactly as they were uncovered by Belzoni a century and a half earlier. Even the upper part of the second statue of Ramesses II from the southern side of the façade of the Great Temple was placed in front of its base, just as it had been found.

A great festival celebrating the salvaging of the Abu Simbel temples took place on September 22, 1968. One reporter present at the event wrote, "everything looks just as it did before; it is enough to make one doubt that the temples were moved at all." On this day, reporters, scientists, Egyptologists, and dignitaries from all over the world came to attend the opening and celebrate this triumph of global cooperation. Egypt thanked the world with precious, monumental gifts (see list below).

The salvage of the two temples raised many conservation problems, so the Egyptian Antiquities Department decided that a permanent conservation laboratory should be set up on the site to protect the temples from any environmental or human hazards. This is a vital part of the salvage effort, since many threats to the monuments still remain. For example, a few months after the inauguration of the new site, a strong storm damaged the nose and parts of the face of one of the statues of Queen Nefertari on the façade of the small temple. Some scholars blamed the damage on the lack of trees in front of the temple (there had been trees on the original site);

Reconstruction of one of the clossal statues of Ramesses II.

others said that extra 60 m (nearly 200 ft) of height protected it from the water, but left the rocks more exposed to the elements.

The Antiquities Department immediately began to plant the area in front of the temples with grass and removed the sand from the temple façades. Unfortunately, they later discovered that the grass attracted insects and snakes and were forced to remove it. One of the other problems that faced the conservators was that the local birds decided that the temple façades made perfect nests, creating a major cleanup problem.

The site of Abu Simbel has become of the most important tourist attractions in Egypt, especially on February 22 and October 22 when the rays of the sun enter the sanctuary of the Great Temple. The city of Abu Simbel has grown enormously and is now connected to Aswan by airplane and boat. There are now about four cruise lines that visit Abu Simbel from Aswan, and a paved road has been built so that the site can be reached by car.

A new magnificent sound and light show, with spectacular music and beautiful scenes projected onto the fronts of the temples, will draw many evening visitors to the site. This project was installed very carefully and caused no damage to the monuments. The story of the show is very romantic; the Nile, the wind, and Ramesses the Great tell the tale of one of the most spectacular periods in history, the Golden Age of Egypt.

Opening celebration for the salvage of the two temples of Abu Simbel.

The monuments of the last Nubian civilization at Meroe.

Nubian Temples Abroad

After the salvage campaign of the Abu Simbel temples under UNESCO, Egypt rewarded many countries with gifts for their generous participation in the project. Five temples were given to various foreign countries and now serve as monumental ambassadors of Egypt. These temples are:

- The Temple of Dabud
- The Temple of Dendur
- The Ptolemaic gate of the temple of Kalabsha
- The Temple of Tafa
- The Temple of el-Lissia

The Temple of Dabud

This temple has stood in the heart of Madrid, the capital of Spain, since 1965. It was built during the Ptolemaic period by the Meroitic king Azkher-Amon (fl. 300 BC) at Dabud, about 20 km (12.5 miles) south of Aswan, on the west bank of the Nile. Many additions were made to the temple in the late Ptolemaic and Roman periods. The temple was dedicated to the god Amun, lord of Thebes and Meroe.

The Temple of Tafa

This temple is now reconstructed inside the Archaeological Museum in Leiden. It was originally built at Tafa about 50 km (30 miles) south of Aswan, not far from Kalabsha. It is a small temple that dates to the Roman period.

The Temple of Dendur

This temple was originally on the west side of the Nile River about 80 km south of Aswan, and was surrounded by houses. It is now located inside

*Temple
of Ramesses II
at el-Sebua.*

the Metropolitan Museum of Art in New York City. It is dated to the Roman period during the reign of the first Roman emperor, Augustus (30 BC). It was dedicated primarily to the two brothers, Badi-Ist and Bahor, sons of the Nubian ruler at the time, but also to the goddess Isis. In the sixth century after Christ, it was converted into a Christian church. The temple was moved to New York in 1965.

Arrival of the blocks of Dendur temple in New York.

The Temple of el-Lissia

Like the temples of Abu Simbel, this very small temple, originally located to the north of Ibrim village, was cut from living rock. It was given to Italy and rebuilt beside the museum of Turin. It dates to the reign of Tuthmoses III (1450 BC) and is dedicated to the god Hôrus lord of Miam (ancient 'Aniba, a site in Nubia), Sesostris III of the Twelfth Dynasty, the god Horus lord of Bohen (also in Nubia), and the goddess Hathor, goddess of Ibshek (in Nubia).

The Ptolemaic Gate
of the Temple of Kalabsha

The temple of Kalabsha was saved by German scholars in 1962–63, under whose guidance it was reassembled 1 km (less than a mile) south of the High Dam. During the disassembly of the temple, they found a great number of stones inside the sanctuary and associated buildings, including 250 blocks with their original colors, about a hundred of them came from a small chapel built by Ptolemy IX (116–110 BC) with further decoration of Augustus. In 1971, a hundred blocks of the great gate of this small chapel, which was composed of a total of 250 blocks, were transferred to the Egyptian Museum in Berlin, to honor German efforts in saving the temple of Kalabsha.

Nineteenth-century drawing of the Pillared Hall of the Great Temple of Abu Simbel.

The sound and light
show at the Great Temple
of Abu Simbel.

Sound and Light at Abu Simbel

In 1980 the Egypt Sound and Light Company was designated by the Egyptian government for sound and light shows at its monuments. Even before that time, the company had produced two shows for ancient sites in Egypt, the first at the Giza Pyramids, which began sound and light shows in 1961, and the second at Karnak in Luxor, beginning in 1972. After the company established a third project at Philae in Aswan, it began to think of a fourth sound and light project of the two temples of Ramesses II and Nefertari at Abu Simbel.

The Egypt Sound and Light Company made all the scientific, engineering, technical, and visibility studies necessary, but the project never got off the ground because the focus was then on upgrading the sound and light projects at the Pyramids and Karnak with new techniques.

The sound and light show at the Temple of Nefertari - Abu Simbel.

The sound and light show at Karnak - Luxor.

Preparation of the Project
at Abu Simbel

In 1999 the company embarked on its Abu Simbel project because the two temples there are renowned, attracting tourists from all over the world. Mr. Muhammad Shafik, head of the company, supervised this project and used the most sophisticated lighting and sound technology. In addition, it was decided that the project should not clash but rather coexist with the monuments and their surroundings. The company cooperated with the Ministry of Culture, the Supreme Council of Antiquities, and the Receiving Company for Housing, Tourism, and Cinema in the making of this project.

The aims of this new sound and light project are:

• To open a new tourist venture in the southern part of Egypt; this sound and light program will be a new technological attraction for both Egyptians and foreign tourists, and it will bring employment and knowledge to the area. It coincides with the Egyptian government's development of new areas of irrigation and settlement in nearby Toshka.

• To increase the number of tourist nights on the site during summer and winter. This, in turn, will increase tourist activities, the development of hotels, and reestablish Nubian crafts in the area.

• To use the site to a greater capacity: many more international and local companies will put Abu Simbel on their tourist itinerary, knowing that there are nighttime activities available. This, in turn, will increase the social and economic importance of the site and of Egypt in general.

• To reaffirm the importance of the development of the town of Abu Simbel. The airport was built to receive private flights and flights in the evening, and the show will increase flight bookings.

• To inaugurate the newly paved and repaired road between Aswan and Abu Simbel.

• To develop the area further and to create more jobs for the local people.

Several steps were taken to ensure favorable development of the project. A scientific committee, composed of the late Dr. Gamal Moukhtar, Dr. Gaballa A. Gaballa, and the author, was appointed to write the script.

The company brought in experts to translate the text into eight languages (Arabic, English, French, German, Italian, Japanese, Russian, and Spanish) and record the show's script in each language. As a result, any person watching the show can simultaneously hear his/her own language via headphones. The same music will be heard by the entire audience.

The show explains the history of Ramesses II, his triumphant victories, his lovely wife Nefertari, and the story of the two temples. The viewer sees the façade of the two temples and the huge statues in the same colors that they were in ancient times. For the first time, visitos are able to witness the sun's rays entering the temples, which without technological apparatus happens only twice a year.

The wind explains the details of the inscriptions of the two temples, which are projected outside the temple for all to see. The viewer will then see scenes of the salvage of the two temples. The show next explains the life of the great king Ramesses II. All the scenes will be images of actual reliefs from inside the temple. I believe this is my most important idea, because in the future this show could entice tourists as an alternative to physically entering the tombs and contributing to their destruction.

Technical Details of the Project

The company's engineers used the most sophisticated techniques for sound; in fact, some were designed especially for this project. Forty actors and actresses were used to record the show in eight languages with experts on music and sound producing the symphonic accompaniment. The engineers also used state-of-the-art lighting technology to produce effects where light appears to be coming from behind and above the temples. The entire show is controlled and run by a computer. The seats were designed for an audience of 400. They are located on the northeastern side of the temple, but are not visible at a distance, and so the panorama of the temples is not affected. The equipment is hidden in wooden boxes, which can be used during the day as seats for visitors to the temple.

The sound and light show at the Great Temple of Abu Simbel.

Nineteenth-century drawing of the Great Temple of Abu Simbel.

Ramesses II: The Story of a Great King

Ramesses II reigned for sixty-seven years, and left behind a legacy of monuments unequalled by any other pharaoh of the New Kingdom. No site in Egypt was untouched by his builders and his monuments: his temples, chapels, statues, and stelae can be found throughout the country. He was a great warrior and diplomat, and he spent much of his reign trying to secure and expand Egypt's borders.

Ramesses the Great ruled during a time of turmoil and change, when empires were rising and falling and the Mediterranean world was in a state of flux. He was the heir to a country just beginning to emerge from the chaos that had overtaken the land at the end of the Eighteenth Dynasty, when the heretic king, Akhenaten, had overthrown the normal order of Egyptian society.

Akhenaten had inherited a prosperous land and a vast empire that had been established under the warrior-kings of the early New Kingdom. During the Old and Middle Kingdoms, Egypt had coexisted with its neighbors in more or less friendly trading relations, but the trauma of the Second Intermediate Period, when the Egyptians had been squeezed between the Hyksos in the north and the Kushites in the south, had left them with a new belligerence. By creating and maintaining a huge empire, the kings of the early New Kingdom were able to guarantee Egypt stability, security, and a thriving economy. Since the reign of Ahmose I at the beginning of the Eighteenth Dynasty, the armies of Egypt had marched out to impose Egyptian influence and power all the way to the Euphrates in the east and south to Napata at Gebel Barkal, deep in the heart of Nubia.

This changed during the rule of Akhenaten, who moved the capital from Thebes to a new city called Amarna, closed all the major temples, and

The tomb of Seti I in the Valley of the Kings - Luxor.

called on the Egyptians to abandon most of the old gods and follow him in the worship of the sun disk, the Aten. This heretic king settled himself within the borders of his new city, Akhetaten, and swore he would never leave it. Neighboring peoples to the north seized this chance to claim many of Egypt's foreign possessions in Syro-Palestine.

Akhenaten was succeeded on the throne by several young and weak kings (including Tutankhamun), who were forced by the old priesthood to abandon Akhenaten's city and religion, move back to Thebes, and reopen the temples.

The last king of the Eighteenth Dynasty was a man named Horemheb, who had been commander-in-chief of the army and king's deputy under

Face from one of the statues of Ramesses II.

Akhenaten. This king brought law and order back to the country by instituting an important series of internal reforms. Akhenaten and his immediate successors were deliberately erased from the pages of Egyptian history. Horemheb and his wife, the princess Mutnodjmet, had no sons to inherit the throne, so the kingship passed to a young army commander named Ramesses, who founded the Nineteenth Dynasty. The future Ramesses I was the son of an army officer named Seti, one of Horemheb's most loyal and dependable statesmen. As a youth, Ramesses joined the army and soon rose to the important post of Commander of the Military Chariots. He then became a diplomatic representative of the king in foreign lands, Commander of the Sile Fortress in the Sinai, and the officer responsible for the protection of the Mediterranean coast. He was later named Minister for the South and the King's Right Arm in Thebes.

Young Ramesses was ambitious, and dedicated himself to carrying out the king's orders faithfully and efficiently. He was rewarded for his loyalty and effectiveness with the title of king's deputy in both the south and north of the land, was named sole heir to the throne of Egypt, and eventually succeeded to the throne as Ramesses I. While he was crown prince, Ramesses and his wife bore a son whom they named Seti. The young Seti (the future Seti I) married a woman named Tuya, daughter of the Commander of the Military Chariots. The young couple lost their first child, but soon had another, who became eternally famous as Ramesses II.

Ramesses II was educated by his father, who trained him in his royal duties. By the time he was 10, Seti had made him titular commander-in-chief of the army, and when he reached the age of 16, he became prince-regent of Egypt, sharing power with his father, who had been on the throne for seven years. An ancient text describes the regency ceremony for us:

> When my father appeared before his people, I still being
> a young man under his wing, he spoke of me thus: 'Let
> him appear as King and let me see his beauty while I still
> live put the big crown on his head . . . he shall rule this
> land and direct its affairs. He shall lead its people' . . .
> Thus he spoke, for he loved me from the depth of his
> heart.

Like all princes of New Kingdom Egypt, Prince Ramesses received a military upbringing. He learned how to fight and how to design military strategies. His father's many wars, fought in foreign lands such as Syria and Libya, became his training ground; while in the field, he learned the arts of defense and attack, how to encircle towers and fortresses, and other military techniques.

In the Year 30 of his father Seti I's rule, Prince-Regent Ramesses led a campaign to Lower Nubia to put down a minor rebellion. He brought with him two of his own sons, aged four and five. In celebration of his victory, he built a small rock-cut temple in Nubia, at Beit el-Wali near Kalabsha. This was the first of a number of monuments he would erect in Nubia, including the temples at Abu Simbel.

Seti I also entrusted his son with major building projects at Abydos, the Karnak Temple, and his own mortuary temple, his Temple of Millions of Years, at Qurna. These early projects helped prepare Ramesses II for a life dedicated to building.

While he was the young heir to the throne, Ramesses took two wives. The first was his principal queen, Nefertari, whose smaller temple sits beside his at Abu Simbel. The second was named Istnofret. By the time he took over sole rule of Egypt, each of his queens had borne him five children. Over the course of his long and prosperous rule, Ramesses had at least six principal queens and a number of lesser queens and concubines and sired almost a hundred children.

The Sole Rule of Ramesses II

In the summer of the year 1279 BC, in the sixteenth year of his reign, Seti I died and Ramesses II officially succeeded to the throne of Egypt. At his coronation he took the name of Son of the Sun, Userma'at-Re-Setepenre, and a series of royal titles: King of Upper and Lower Egypt, Ramesses Beloved of Amun, Horus the Powerful Bull, Horus the Golden, Beloved of the Goddesses Wadjet and Nekhbet.

Upon assuming the throne, Ramesses II began an unprecedented campaign of construction that would last for the entire six and a half decades of his reign. There is no place in Egypt that does not show some remnants of Ramesses II's construction efforts. He built himself a grand mortuary temple, the Ramesseum, across the river from Thebes. He built a spectacular temple at Abydos, the two temples at Abu Simbel, the temples at Beit el-Wali, and two temples in the Valley of the Lions in Lower Nubia. He added two halls, a lofty chapel, and two obelisks to the Luxor Temple. He finished a huge 152-column hypostyle hall that was begun by his father Seti in the Karnak temple. During his long and prosperous reign, Ramesses II also left statues and other likenesses of himself all over the land.

He considered his building work to be sacred tasks entrusted to him by the gods. This text shows his pride in his work:

> He is the kind god Ramesses who achieved knowledge
> and writing equal to that of the God Thoth; he understands
> what is, and knows how man conducts himself. After
> perusing the register of the House of Life and after
> knowing the secrets of the sky and the hidden truths of
> earth . . . I am the one whose hands construct useful
> works . . . I have decided to achieve the projects of the
> God Amun and build the constructions in his temple
> south of Thebes.

Recent excavation at Giza has revealed an unfinished large double statue of Ramesses II as a king and as a god. This is actually the first time that a statue for this king has been found at Giza. From the same period comes an inscription of the architect of Ramesses, May, which he left on the stones of the second pyramid. I believe that May wanted to sculpt a double statue for the king to be erected at Heliopolis. He did not want to go all the way to the main granite quarry at Aswan, so instead he used granite casing blocks that had fallen from the façade of the Third Pyramid. However, the sculptors made a mistake and broke the statue in the middle, so May left it where it lay for us to discover.

It is amazing how much building activity was carried out by this king all over Egypt. Recently, Kent Weeks found a tomb known as KV5 in the

Valley of the Kings. Weeks believes that this tomb was used for the burial of the children of Ramesses II. My own theory is that this tomb was a cenotaph, a mock burial, for the family of Ramesses, designed to associate them with the god Osiris, whose rock-cut statue dominates the interior of the tomb. The chapels inside the tomb are very small, and would not fit a sarcophagus. No bones have been found that could be the remains of these princes, and we know that many of the children of Ramesses were buried elsewhere.

Ramesses II inherited a land where many of the old monuments had fallen into disrepair. He spent much time and energy restoring ancient buildings, and completed many of the monuments left unfinished by the kings who had gone before him. When he visited Abydos in the first year of his rule to see how work was progressing on his temple, he left a text that expressed his dismay at what he found there:

Ramesses II in the presence of the gods.

He saw the deterioration of the buildings and tombs in the cemetery of the previous kings at Abydos. Some were falling apart, others had not been completed, walls were crumbling or left unfinished, stones were falling out, and the buildings were incomplete. When the kings died their sons and heirs did not complete or repair their fathers' monuments in the cemetery. The front and back of the Temple of Men-Ma'at-Re [his father, Seti I] were still under construction when he died. His monuments were not completed and the columns did not rise on their stands. The statues, unsculpted, lay on the ground

The Ramesseum Temple - West Thebes .

*"no offerings were made, and even his priests served no
longer and the fields were robbed"*

Faced with this lamentable situation, Ramesses II called his men and
spoke to them:

*Look, I have called you to tell you my thoughts. The
noblest act is to honor those who left his world and a
son should honor and commemorate his father. I have
decided to make offerings to Men-Ma'at-Re [Seti I] so
that it may be forever said: 'his son made his name
eternal. May Osiris bless my father and may his son the
Pharaoh have a long life.'*

The text continues:

*His majesty gave his orders to the managers of the
workshops, and told his soldiers and workers and
sculptors to build his father's temple and to repair and
restore all destruction in the cemetery.*

Ramesses II also erased the names of previous kings from many monuments and replaced them with his own cartouches. For example, one
researcher has suggested the colossal statues of Ramesses II in Memphis
were originally Old Kingdom statues of King Khafra that were usurped by
a Middle Kingdom ruler and then reusurped by Ramesses II. It has often
been stated that this sort of activity was evidence of his megalomania, that
he was claiming all the monuments as his own. However, others think that
by putting his own name, the name of the undisputed ruler of the land, on
older monuments, he was protecting them from harm.

Among his many projects was the construction of a new city in the
Delta, Per Ramesses. According to one text:

*His Majesty built himself a city called the City of Great
Victories between Syria and Egypt, rich with food and
supplies like Thebes, eternal as Memphis, the sun shines
in its skies and sets in its horizons. All left their cities and
settled there.*

This became a city pulsing with noise, movement, and action. Egyptians
and foreigners alike converged on it to enjoy its beauty and the magnifi-
cence of its celebrations. The joys of Per Ramesses were evident in the
souls of its inhabitants who enjoyed its natural beauty and gardens as they
sang love songs.

Foreign Affairs

As soon as he had gained control of internal affairs, Ramesses II began to look outward. He inherited from his grandfather and father a military spirit and expansionist ambitions, as well as a desire to spread Egypt's influence. He followed the example set by his two predecessors, who had rushed to mount campaigns in Syria to recover the territory that had been lost in the aftermath of the Amarna period.

As soon as Ramesses II mounted the throne, the Delta was subjected to waves of attack from the People of the Sea, a motley group of raiders who had been squeezed out of their homelands and were searching for new places to settle. He fought them and pushed them back; many of the prisoners he took in these battles became mercenaries in his army.

Ramesses II immortalized his defense of Egypt and his victory over the Peoples of the Sea on a rock in Aswan. This is dated to Year 2 of his reign and says: The fighters of the sea were destroyed and the Delta slept in peace. The inscription also reports that Ramesses II destroyed the foreign people of the north and that the Tehnu (Libyans) fell back in fear of him. A tablet from Tanis, east of the Delta, refers to his occupation of western lands, which could have allied themselves with the Shardana, one of the groups that formed the Peoples of the Sea. To immortalize his early exploits in Nubia, there are scenes of the king fighting Nubians in his temples at Beit el-Wali and Abu Simbel.

Ramesses II smites enemies with a mace in front of the god Khnum - Temple of El-Sebua.

Ramesses II smites enemies with a mace in front of the god Amun-Re - Abu Simbel.

Ramesses II's reputation as a great warrior is based mainly on his northern campaigns, which occupied him for his entire reign. His goal at the outset of his reign was to retake the Syrian coastline, restore the Egyptian colony at Amor, reconquer the city of Qadesh, and continue up the coast to Aleppo. In the fourth year of his reign, he led his first campaign into Syria to secure the cities of the Phoenician coast, and spent two months reconquering Sur, Djebeil, and Arkata before moving east to confront the Amurru, whom he defeated handily.

In Year 5, Ramesses fought one of the decisive battles of his reign, a battle whose outcome would set the terms of war and peace for the next century and establish him as a great warrior-king. This was the battle of Qadesh, in which the young king faced his most powerful foe, the Hittite king Muwutallis. Qadesh was a key city that had historically been held by the Egyptians, but was lost during the reign of Akhenaten. Seti I had won it back, only to give it up again in a peace treaty with the Hittites. Ramesses II was determined to take back the city and restore the former glory of the Egyptian empire. The great irony of this battle is that it was actually a draw, and the Egyptians were saved from complete disaster only by the personal heroism of Ramesses himself.

Ramesses immortalized this battle and the role that he played in it, both in text and in pictures on the walls of his temples at Karnak, Luxor, his mortuary temple (the Ramesseum), Abydos, and Abu Simbel. The Egyptian account is also preserved in hieratic on three ancient papyri.

According to the Egyptian version of the story, the Hittite army under King Muwutallis was composed of soldiers from sixteen regions divided into two regiments of 1,800 and 1,900 soldiers as well as 2,500 military chariots.

Ramesses himself describes the Egyptian army:

> *His majesty prepared his troops and his chariots as well as the mercenaries he had previously taken prisoner and explained his campaign plan. The march started well in the fifth year of his reign, the second month of the sun season, on the ninth day. Ramesses II divided his army into four regiments named Amun, Re, Ptah, and Set. He himself led the Amun regiment.*

The other three regiments were under the command of princes of the royal house. The plan was for the Amun regiment, under Ramesses II, to advance by land to Canaan, then through the south of Syria to the city of Qadesh. The other regiments would take other routes and meet with the main force under the king's command near the city.

The main force of the Egyptian army made camp 25 km (16 miles) from Qadesh. The next morning, the regiment moved on to the town of Shebtona on the eastern bank of the Orontes River. During this march, two men from the Shasu Bedouin tribe came to declare their loyalty and their ruler's loyalty to the pharaoh of Egypt, claiming that they had broken off relations with the Hittites. Ramesses II asked: Where are your rulers? The two men answered that they were with the Hittite king and that the Hittites were in Aleppo north of Tuneb. Muwutallis, they said, was afraid to advance southward since he had learned that the pharaoh was moving north. According to the Bedouin, the Hittites were camped 200 km (125 miles) from Qadesh. This information encouraged Ramesses II to advance speedily toward the city at the head of the Amun regiment, leaving the Re, Ptah, and Set regiments to catch up later. Ramesses and his troops crossed the Shebtona and moved to Qadesh without waiting for the rest of the army.

When Ramesses reached the outskirts of Qadesh, just northwest of the city, the Re regiment was just crossing the Shebtona River, the Ptah regiment was south of Aronama (about 22 km, or 14 miles, west of Qadesh), and the Set regiment was still on the road. Ramesses set up camp to wait for the rest of the troops. While he was waiting, his soldiers captured two enemy spies, who confessed that the Hittite army was not at Aleppo at all, but was, in fact, in position just northeast of Qadesh! Ramesses realized that he had walked into a trap, and sent his minister to urge the Ptah regiment to come quickly to his aid. Advance quickly, the message read, your master the Pharaoh stands alone in battle.

The Hittite king chose a good time to attack the Egyptian army. As the Re regiment crossed the Shebtona River, the king, Muwutallis, launched a surprise attack, driving his 2,500 war chariots against them. The Egyptians were in no position to fight back; the soldiers panicked and broke rank, some heading for the Ptah regiment to their south and others running north toward Amun and their pharaoh. The Hittites followed those going north, harrying them until they reached the camp of the Amun regiment. When the Hittites reached the Amun camp, they overran it, and most of the troops fled, leaving only Ramesses himself, a handful of officers and men, and his personal bodyguard. Pharaoh and his men fought back courageously and held their ground. Some of those who had fled returned when they saw that the Hittites were being pushed back, and a strong nucleus of fierce resistance was formed.

Ramesses II and his troops pierced the ranks of the Hittites and marched south to meet with his Ptah regiment. At this dangerous moment, help arrived in the form of a regiment of young men, the Na'arin (Strong Youths), whom Ramesses had ordered to protect the coastal road and meet the army at Qadesh. The arrival of this regiment had a magical influence—the balance of power changed in favor of the Egyptians and the

Ramesses II on his chariot smites enemies in the battle of Qadesh - Abu Simbel.

Ramesses II smites enemies with a mace in front of the god Re-Horakhti - Abu Simbel.

Hittite chariots gave way before them. Muwutallis sent another 1,000 chariots into the battle, but they were helpless before the strength and bravery of the Egyptian army.

The Egyptian army followed the guiding spirit of their king, a warrior who never gave up, and defeated the enemy, whose troops fled and threw themselves into the Orontes River. The Ptah regiment finally arrived, and soon the Egyptian forces had full control of the area.

On the next day, there were skirmishes between the two armies, but neither force was able to settle matters decisively. According to Egyptian texts, the Hittite king sent messengers to pharaoh asking for a truce and cessation of hostilities. Ramesses convened his advisors and put the Hittite proposal to them. They said: "Peace is a great thing and above all else, your Majesty. No one can oppose a settlement. If you so wish it, who can withstand your anger?" Ramesses accepted the truce in hope of seizing Qadesh at a later date.

Although it is clear that the battle of Qadesh was not an outright Egyptian victory, the scenes that Ramesses ordered carved on the walls of his temples show him victorious over his enemy. The reason is that these drawings represent not just this specific battle between the Egyptians and Hittites, but the eternal battle for order over chaos. The Egyptian king, as the earthly manifestation of the creator god, must always be shown as victorious, thus ensuring the proper functioning of the Egyptian universe.

As soon as Ramesses II had returned home, the cities along the Syro-Palestinian coast rose in rebellion against him. Muwutallis seized one city after another, including Amurru and Qadesh. In the years that followed, Ramesses continued to mount campaigns into Syria, retaking many of the cities that had been lost. These battles reestablished Egyptian rule in the area, but the fierce and constant struggles between Egypt and the Hittites depleted the two sides at a time when a new power was emerging on the scene: the Assyrians under the leadership of King Adad-nirari I. This new empire took over the remnants of the territory of the Mitanni east of the Euphrates and became a serious threat to the Hittites.

At the same time, Egypt was under further attacks by the Peoples of the Sea. The Egyptians and the Hittites realized that they could no longer afford to fight one another, and decided to sign a peace treaty. In Year 21 of Ramesses II's reign, two messengers from the Hattusil III, then king of the Hittites, arrived carrying a silver tablet on which was written a request for a new treaty of peace.

The text of the treaty reads:

> *Look, for Hattusil the great prince of the Hittites has agreed with Userma'at-Re-Setepenre [Ramesses II], the Great Ruler of Egypt, that from this day forward there shall be a good peace between us and eternal brotherhood—he is in brotherhood and peace with me and I am in brotherhood and peace with him for eternity.*

> *Look, I, the Great Prince of the Hittites, am in brotherhood and peace with the sons of Ramesses-Mery-Amun and this peace. The land of Egypt and the land of the Hittites shall live like us in peace and brotherhood always, and never shall there by enmity between them.*

The text continues, outlining the terms of the peace, which included a mutual defense pact. This is one of the earliest treaties to have survived from ancient times.

The family of Ramesses II

History—and Ramesses' own penchant for building—has preserved a significant amount of information about the family of this great king. Chief among the women at his court was his mother, Queen Tuya, to whom he was devoted. The other principal women of the court were Nefertari and Istnofret, both women whom he married before his ascension as sole ruler to the throne. Each of these queens bore him many children who were of great help to him in ruling the land. Queen Nefertari bore him his eldest son, Amun-hir-Wonmef, whose name was later changed to Amun-hir-Khopshef, four more sons, and two girls, Merit-Amun and Merit-Atum. Queen Istnofret bore the princes Ramesses, Khaemwaset, Merenptah, and the princess Bint-Anat.

The monuments of Queen Nefertari suggest that she was a very beautiful woman. Though it has not been proven that she was of royal blood, she was Ramesses II's chief wife and appeared beside him on public occasions and official and religious ceremonies. During the first twenty years of his reign, her statues were often placed side by side with his. He built a tomb for her in the Valley of the Queens which remains one of the most beautiful and famous of the tombs in the Valley.

Nefertari had many titles that show not only her official standing, but also the love and esteem that her husband had for her. She was Lady of Upper and Lower Egypt and the Delta, Lady of All Lands, the Greatly Praised One, the Beautiful of Face, Goddess of Charm, and the Sweetest in Love.

To show his great love for her, Ramesses II built a temple for Nefertari next to his Great Temple at Abu Simbel. Nefertari was portrayed in this temple in the form of Hathor. One inscription on the temple reads: Ramesses built a temple dug in the rock so that it may remain eternally for Queen Nefertari the Beloved in Nubia, Nefertari for whom the sun rises. Her presence at the signing of the peace treaty with the Hittites is proof of the high esteem in which she was held by her husband.

Queen Istnofret was also very high in Ramesses II's favor, although she remained second to Nefertari for most of his reign. She does appear as First Queen, with her sons and daughters, on an edifice in Aswan, and on a second memorial that shows her and her daughter serving King Ramesses while Prince Khaemwaset stands before him. She apparently died in the thirty-fourth year of his reign and was buried in the Valley of the Queens, but her tomb has not yet been found.

One of Ramesses II's lesser queens was his younger sister, Hent-mi-Re, whom he married in keeping with the Eighteenth Dynasty tradition of uniting male and female heirs to the throne and keeping the royal blood in the family. Hent-mi-Re never played an important role and participated very little in public life.

*Queen Nefertari
from her tomb
in the Valley of the
Queens - Luxor.*

It is possible that Ramesses also married two of his daughters, Bint-Anat and Merit-Amun, both of whom bore the title of Senior Royal Wife. This may, however, have been an honorary title given to them after the deaths of their mothers.

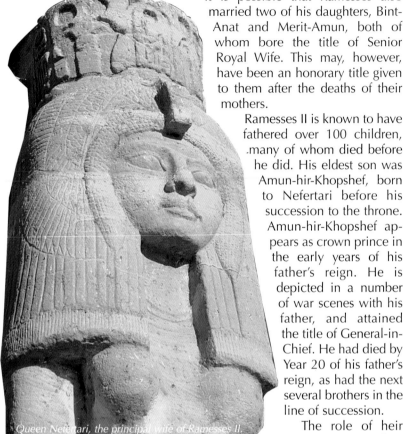

Ramesses II is known to have fathered over 100 children, many of whom died before he did. His eldest son was Amun-hir-Khopshef, born to Nefertari before his succession to the throne. Amun-hir-Khopshef appears as crown prince in the early years of his father's reign. He is depicted in a number of war scenes with his father, and attained the title of General-in-Chief. He had died by Year 20 of his father's reign, as had the next several brothers in the line of succession.

Queen Nefertari, the principal wife of Ramesses II.

The role of heir apparent was then passed to a much younger son of Nefertari, Set-hir-Khopshef, who was the high priest of his father's cult and a special minister of state for the north. This prince appears with his father in scenes depicted the signing of the peace treaty with the Hittites in Year 21. But he also died before his father, probably in about Year 25.

All of Nefetertari's sons seem to have died by this time, and the succession passed to the eldest son of Istnofret, named Ramesses, who held this position from about Year 25 to Year 50. He was followed by his brother Khaemwaset, who appears with his father in many battle scenes. This prince, however, was less interested in war than in intellectual pursuits such as reading, writing, and magic. He entered the service of Ptah at Memphis, where he redesigned the tombs for the sacred Apis bulls (in the catacombs now known as the Serapeum) and built the Temple of Apis. He has also come down through history as the first Egyptologist: he visited the pyramid fields at Giza and Saqqara and cleared and restored many of the monuments there. Among his many triumphs was his father's *sed* festival, or jubilee, celebrated in the thirtieth year of the reign, which he organized and directed. Unfortunately, he outlived his older brother by only five years, and died in Year 55 of his father's reign, at which time he was buried in a tomb inside the Serapeum.

Finally, the succession passed to a younger son of Ramesses II and Istnofret, Merneptah, who managed to outlive his father and succeed to the throne. He claimed the titles of Crown Prince, First among Princes, and Eldest Son of the King (he had begun life as the thirteenth!) and served as the right hand of Ramesses the Great in his later years.

The Egyptians kept the memory of their great King alive in their hearts, just as the earth preserved his monuments and statues. Ramesses II remained a mythical hero to the ancient Egyptians, and was the highest example for all the kings who followed him. Most of the kings after him were named Ramesses, from Ramesses III through Ramesses XI.

Ramesses III, who founded the Twentieth Dynasty, considered Ramesses II to be his sacred hero. He named all of his children after the children of Ramesses II, built a new quarter in the capital city of Per Ramesses in the Delta, and built his own mortuary temple, Medinet Habu, along the lines of the Ramesseum, Ramesses II's mortuary temple. In his own temple, he even added a special altar for the worship of Ramesses II.

Ramesses IV prayed to the gods to extend his reign to sixty-six years like the reign of his hero. The title Userma'at-Re-Setepenre became an essential part of the names of the kings of the Twenty-second and Twenty-third Dynasties, and princes and minor statesmen were proud to claim the lofty title, Son of the King, Son of Ramesses.

The Goddess Ma'at - tomb of Queen Nefertari - Luxor.

Ramesses II
the Divine Pharaoh

Since time immemorial, the ancient Egyptians had a strong conviction that the kingship was a sacred trust passed down to men from the gods who ruled before them. According to myth, the first to rule over humankind was the god Re. When Re became old, there were some who made fun of him, so he rose to the sky and sent his daughter Hathor to avenge him. He left the god Osiris on earth as his heir to the throne. Osiris was killed by his brother Seth, but left behind a posthumous son, Horus, who challenged his uncle's right to the throne. Horus and Seth fought over the kingship for many years, and eventually Horus won and gained his birthright.

The Egyptian pharaoh was considered the embodiment of Horus on earth and son of the sun god Re. Serving in this sacred role, the king provides a bridge between the earthly sphere and the world of the gods. The pharaoh had a double nature: he is human while on earth, but after death becomes united with the gods and is worshipped as a god in his mortuary temple.

During the New Kingdom, adherents of the god Amun became very powerful, posing a threat to the royal house. In response, the kings of the Eighteenth Dynasty exerted every effort to strengthen the worship of other gods, such as Re and Ptah, and put special emphasis on the worship of the living pharaoh.

To instill widespread belief in the divine nature of the pharaoh, these rulers took the following steps:

- They built large temples in Nubia and Egypt dedicated to the worship of the living king
- They linked the pharaoh with the other gods in their temples
- They placed enormous statues of the pharaoh in front of and inside the temples of the gods, inscribing on them names that expressed their divinity. For example, the statue of Amenhotep III in Karnak is called Neb-Ma'at-Re-Montu. Thus, the king (whose throne name was Neb-Ma'at-Re) has been conflated with the god of war, Montu.

Ramesses II, the Divine Pharaoh - Abu Simbel.

In order to become a god, the king had certain duties, given to him at his coronation by the gods, that he was obliged to carry out. These duties were to build a tomb for himself, build temples for the gods, defeat Egypt's enemies, present offerings to the gods, and guarantee the unity of the two regions of Egypt.

Achieving all these goals raised the pharaoh to the stature of a god. Ramesses II was the most energetic of pharaohs in his quest to fulfill his sacred duties during his lifetime. He thought of himself as a sacred king with close links to the gods; he called on them and they responded. Monumental inscriptions from his reign are full of examples of his personal relations with the gods.

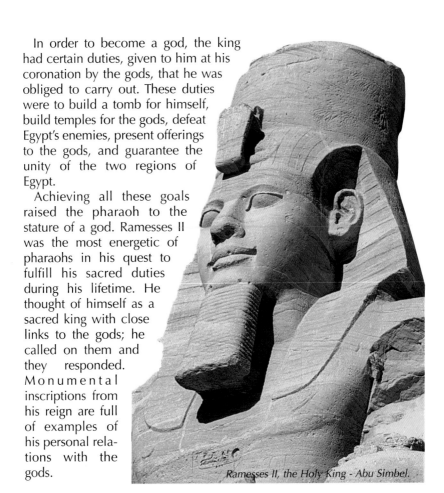
Ramesses II, the Holy King - Abu Simbel.

During the battle of Qadesh, he pleaded to the god Amun for help, and Amun saved him. He then called upon the god Seth, praying that there be no rain or ice during the voyage of his Hittite bride to Egypt. Seth responded and the sky stayed clearwinter became summer. One of Ramesses' men gives credit for the safe arrival of the princess, her retinue, and the Egyptian delegation to the god-king Ramesses II, saying, the reason is that the sky is under his thumb and does his will.

When Ramesses II sent a mining mission to the remote hills in the Eastern Desert of Nubia in the Eastern Desert to extract gold from its mountains, the workers faced a major problem due to the scarcity of water. In fact, it was on this account that none of the preceding pharaohs had been able to extract the gold from these areas. Ramesses II planned a series of wells along the desert routes to obtain sufficient water for his mission. The men of his court came to him and said:

You are like Re in all you do, whatever your heart desires must happen. If during the nighttime you wish for something, as soon as dawn breaks you have your wish. If you tell water to gush from the mountain so shall it happen, plentifully, as though you were Re himself. . . . These lands have lacked water from the beginning of time and people there die of thirst, but if you tell your father the god of the Nile. 'Let water spring from the mountain,' he shall answer you and do as you want.

Ramesses II consolidated his godly state by building numerous temples in which he was worshipped in the image of the different gods. He linked his funeral temple, the Ramesseum, to the temples of the god Amun. At his temple in Abydos he likened himself to the god Osiris. In his temple at Abu Simbel, he associated himself with the sun god, Re-Horakhti, and with Ptah and Amun-Re. He also built two other Nubian temples in the Valley of the Lions, one dedicated to the King as Amun and the other as Ptah. Thus, the three gods of the empire, Amun, Re, and Ptah were embodied by Ramesses II.

Parallel with the construction of these temples, magnificent statues of Ramesses were sculpted everywhere to reinforce his divinity. At Aksha in Nubia he erected an enormous statue that was dedicated by him to "Ramesses the Great God, God of Nubia." His capital, Per Ramesses, teemed with statues that described him as "Montu in the Two Regions," The God," the "Brightest among Gods," "Beloved of Atum," "Spirit of the Great Re-Horahkti," "Son of Kings" or "King of Kings." These statues were placed in the front walls of temples so as to be seen by all.

Thus, the beautiful temples at Abu Simbel represent a magnificent paean to Ramesses the Great and his beautiful Queen Nefertari as gods. He was worshipped there, by Nubians and Egyptians, during his lifetime and after his death. After lying hidden beneath the sands for centuries, the temples are once again serving their original purpose, bringing eternal life to their builder and his consort.

Nineteenth-century drawing
of the sanctuary
of the Great Temple of Abu Simbel.

The Temples of Abu Simbel

In 1290 BC, Ramesses the Great carved two unique temples into the rocks of Abu Simbel, 280 km (175 miles) south of Aswan in a remote and isolated part of Lower Nubia. Neolithic rock drawings and tools found at the site suggest that it gained importance as early as the prehistoric era. An earlier chapel to a local image of Horus also stood on the site.

The façade of the Great Temple of Abu Simbel.

The two temples were carved into bluffs of pinkish sandstone rising steeply from the desert bordering the narrow floodplain of the Nile. Behind the temples stretches the vast African desert. The temples face east to receive the rays of the rising sun. It is still a mystery to archaeologists how the ancient Egyptians could have designed and built such miraculous structures—how they could have known that they could dig 60 m (197 ft) into the living rock without encountering any faults in the stone?

The site enjoys a very special relation to the goddess Hathor, goddess of beauty and love in ancient Egypt, and her father Re. Dedicated to Queen Nefertari as Hathor, the smaller northern temple lies at about 122 m (400 ft) above sea level. The great southern temple, slightly higher at 124 m about sea level, is dedicated to Ramesses II as the sun god Re-Horakhti.

These two temples are some of the most remarkable achievements of the ancient world, only slightly less impressive than the Great Pyramid of Khufu. As noted above, they were first seen by modern Western eyes in 1813, by Burckhardt, but it was not until the UNESCO Salvage Campaign that they became one of the most popular sites for travelers to Egypt.

The Great Temple

The southern temple (see plan page 75) was built in Year 34 of Ramesses II's reign and dedicated to Re-Horakhti, Amun, Ptah, and Ramesses himself as god-king. In front of the temple is a forecourt, guarded on the north by a wall pierced by a single gateway (**1**). The enormous pylon-shaped façade of the temple, which measures 38 m (125 ft) wide and 13 m (43 ft) high, is cut back into the pinkish stone of the cliff. Steps lead up to a ledge decorated with sculptures of falcons as symbols of the sun god and mummiform statues of Ramesses II as Osiris. This ledge extends across the façade of the temple, in front of four colossal seated figures of Ramesses the Great.

All four statues show Ramesses seated with his hands flat on his knees, bare-chested, and wearing the royal kilt, with a *nemes* headdress and the double crown of united Egypt on his head. Standing at the feet of these statues are images of eleven members of the king's family. From left to right, these are: the princesses Nebet-Tawi and Bint-Anat; an unknown woman who may be Queen Istnofret; the Queen Mother Tuya; Queen Nefertari; Crown Prince Amun-hir-khopshef; Queen Nefertari (again); Prince Ramesses; Queen Tuya; Nefertari (again); and finally, Princess Merit-Amun.

The sides of the two thrones on which the colossal statues sit are decorated with images of the god Hapi, god of the Nile, who performs the *sema-tawy,* the symbolic uniting of the two lands, tying the lotus of Upper Egypt and the papyrus of Lower Egypt around the hieroglyph for *unite.*

Part of the façade of the Great Temple of Abu Simbel.

Below the thrones are engraved the nine bows, symbols of the traditional enemies of Egypt. Above the entrance is a niche containing a statue of the god Re-Horakhti, who carries an *user* staff in one hand and the feather of Ma'at, goddess of truth, in the other. On his head is the sun disk of Re. This statue is thus an elaborate form of the king's name: User-Ma'at-Re. Along the top of the temple façade is a row of baboons in eternal prayer to the rising sun.

There are a number of ancient graffiti left by Greek and Semitic travelers inscribed on the surface of the temple. For example, on the left leg of the second statue on the southern side is a graffito in Greek, left by one of the soldiers sent by King Psametik II of the Twenty-sixth Dynasty to Nubia in the early part of the sixth century BC. The temple was later covered with sand, and I believe that this is the reason that it was not chosen to be one of the Seven Wonders of the Ancient World.

In 1884, about 3,000 years after the construction of the temple, an Egyptian army that included some British soldiers passed through, just as Psametik's troops had done 2,000 years earlier. They were on their way to stop a revolution in the Sudan. In front of the temple, the expedition left a stelae inscribed with this information. They also buried one of their comrades in this area.

Marriage with the Hittite princess

At the southern edge of the temple façade is inscribed a document describing the marriage of Ramesses II to a Hittite princess (**2**). This marriage was a diplomatic one, designed to consolidate the ties of peace and friendship between the two countries. This document describes the arrival of the princess in Egypt:

> *Look, for the King of the Hittites has sent his daughter in a rich cavalcade that fills the road from side to side. The princess and the notables of the Kingdom of Kheta have crossed high mountains and difficult roads until they reached the borders of Syria, which is under your rule.*

> *Look, as the daughter of the great King of the Hittites entered Egypt, she was surrounded by the soldiers of the Egyptian army and its chariots and his Majesty's men who mixed with the soldiers and chariots and notables of the Hittite Kingdom. They ate and drank together, united like brothers, peace prevailed among them and friendship, thus finding an example in the God Ramesses II. Wherever the procession marched, kings and statesmen cowered in fear at the sight of the people of Kheta united with the people of Egypt.*

Statue of god Re-Horakhti in niche above the entrance of the Great Temple.

As the princess enters the palace of the Pharaoh, the text continues:

> The procession has reached Per Ramesses, and the
> daughter of the great King of the Hittites has entered into
> the presence of the Pharaoh with her great gift box full
> of rich presents. His Majesty looked at her and she was
> beautiful. This is a great event that the Egyptians have
> never known, folk tales mention it not, nor was there
> any mention in writings since the time of our ancient
> forefathers. The daughter of the great ruler of Kheta
> advanced to the heart of Egypt to meet Ramesses. She
> pleased his Majesty and he loved her more than anything
> else. It was a great event for him and a great victory given
> to him by Ptah-Tatanen. He announced that forthwith her
> Egyptian name was Ma'at-Hor-Nefru-Re.

This queen became very important; she is shown with the king in a
number of reliefs and on numerous statues. Her diplomatic importance
is summed up in this inscription: from now on, if a man or woman trav-
els to Syria for any reason, they can reach the land of the Hittites without any fear as a result of his Majesty's victories.

The entrance to the temple leads to a corridor whose walls are
engraved with images of Ramesses II presenting sacrificial plates to the
god Re-Horakhti and the goddess Weret-Hekau (**3**).

Great Pillared Hall (4)

At the end of this corridor is a door decorated with cartouches of
Ramesses II and a depiction of the king before Re-Horakhti and the gods
Sekhmet, Amun-Re, and Nut. Ramesses presents a piece of cloth to Amun
and flowers to Re-Horakhti. This door leads to a hall 20 m (66 ft) long and
18 m (59 ft) wide whose ceiling is supported by eight square columns. On
their sides overlooking the central walkway are carved statues of the king.
Those on the south side wear the white crown of Upper Egypt, those on
the north the red crown of Lower Egypt.

Columns on the left

On the columns to the left as one enters the hall, Ramesses II carved a
description of the building of the temple of Ptah in Memphis in Year 34 of
his reign. On these columns are also the following figures: On the first, the
king burns incense before an image of himself as a god; on the second,

The Pillared Hall of the Great Temple of Abu Simbel.

Queen Nefertari burns incense before Hathor, goddess of Ibshek; on the third, the king presents flowers to the god Min and incense to Isis. On the second column, Ramesses II presents the Ma'at feather (symbol of truth and justice) to the god Amun-Re and presents incense and sacrifices to the god Ptah, bread to the god Sobek-Re, and flowers to Amun-Re. The reliefs on the third column portray the king presenting a plate of offerings to Re-Horakhti, sacrifices to Amun-Re, and incense to Osiris. The fourth column has similar scenes, but it is now in poor condition.

Columns on the right

The columns on the right in the great pillared hall have the following decoration: on the first column, the king presents the Ma'at feather to the god Shu; on the second, he presents offerings to Horus, the god of Baki, and flowers to the god Mut; on the third, he presents flowers to the god Djehuty, bread to Amun-Re, flowers to Horus of the city of Ha, bread to Anubis, offerings to the god Khnum, the Ma'at feather to Amun-Re and flowers to Re-Horakhti. The fourth column, now in poor condition, had similar presentation scenes.

The ceiling between the two lines of columns is decorated with an image of the vulture goddess Nekhbet spreading her wings; the two sides of the ceiling are decorated with stars.

Drawings on the walls of the hall

The eastern wall is dominated by a drawing of the king with eight of his sons smiting Nubian and Hittite prisoners in the presence of the god Amun. A second image shows the king with his *ka*, or double, and eight of his daughters smiting prisoners before the god Re-Horakhti. Below the carving the artist has signed his work: engraved by Meri-Amun-bia, son of Kha-Nefer.

The southern wall of the hall shows the king burning incense on the top half and scenes of the king's wars in Nubia, Libya, and Syria, including one depiction of Ramesses attacking a Syrian fortress, on the lower half.

On the western wall, the king drives two columns of Nubian prisoners into the presence of Amun-Re and two columns of Syrian prisoners before Re-Horakhti.

The northern wall of the hall portrays events from the battle of Qadesh in the following order: the advance of the Ptah regiment and the king in his military chariot; the city of Qadesh; the king again in his chariot; the battle of the military chariots; the two spies being captured and questioned; the camp and military chariots and assistance arriving to support the Egyptian army.

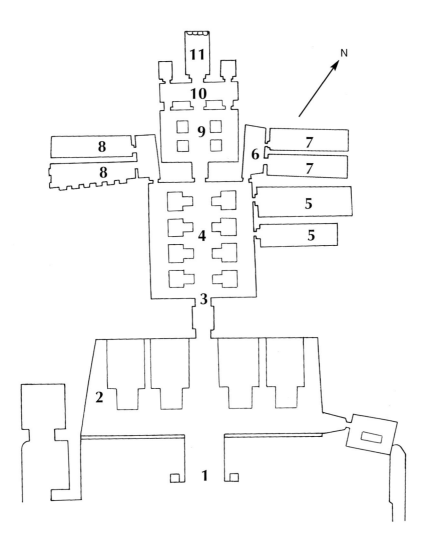

Plan of the Great Temple

Ramesses II smites enemies with a mace in front of the god Amun-Re - Abu Simbel.

Storerooms

Doors in the northern wall of the hall open into two rooms (**5**) that appear to have been used as storerooms for the temple. Their walls are decorated with images of the king in the presence of Hathor, Isis, Re-Horakhti, Amun-Re, Ptah, Khonsu, and Ma'at.

Doors in the north and south ends of the western wall lead to two foyers, each of which leads into two additional rooms. The walls of the northwestern foyer (**6**) are decorated with drawings of the king presenting offerings to Djehuti and Amun-Re, the triumvirate of Thebes (Amun, Mut, and Khonsu), and Montu, Isis, and Re.

The walls of the two northwestern rooms (**7**) are decorated with images of the king before the gods Ma'at, Webwawat, Amun-Re, Khnum, Ptah, Djehuti, and Montu. Four small cows are led before Khnum, and cloth, plates, sacrifices and paint are presented to the gods.

The walls of the southwestern rooms (**8**) are decorated with scenes of a religious nature. On the walls of the northern room, the king bows before Amun-Re and the goddess Mut; on the northern side, Ramesses II presents offerings to the god Min, while on the southern side, he presents wine to the god Ptah.

Second Pillared Hall (9)

In the center of the western wall of the great pillared hall (moving in a straight line as one enters from outdoors through the hall) is a doorway leading to a second, smaller room. Originally at its entrance were carved two sphinxes and a headless sandstone statue of Bissior II, ruler of Kush; all of these statues are now in the British Museum. This room is almost a perfect square, its ceiling resting on four square-cut columns. The walls and columns are decorated with religious scenes: the king presenting flowers to Amun-Re and Mut; the king and Queen Nefertari advancing towards the god Amun-Re; the king before Amun-Re and Re-Horakhti; the king and queen before the bark of the divine Ramesses II; and the King presenting lettuce to Amun-Re and Isis.

Vestibule (10)

From an opening in the center of the western wall of the second pillared hall we enter the vestibule, a broad hall, longer from north to south, perhaps used to present offerings, such as the wine, fruit, and flowers depicted on the walls. There are also scenes showing the king before himself as a god; the king receiving the ankh, the symbol of life, from Amun-Re and from himself as a god; and the king presenting wine to Horus, incense to Amun-Re, and flowers to Ptah.

The western wall of this room has three doors. The doors at the two sides each lead to a small undecorated storage chamber; the center door leads to the inner sanctuary.

Sanctuary (11)

Dominating the *sanctum sanctorum* is a niche in the western wall containing four rock-cut statues, from left to right, of Ptah, Amun-Re, Ramesses II as a god, and Re-Horakhti. The choice of these particular gods can be interpreted to show the political and religious balance of power among the cities of Heliopolis (the city of Re-Horakhti), Memphis (the city of Ptah), Thebes (the city of Amun-Re), and Per-Ramesses (the city of Ramesses himself). A broken base in the center of the room would have held the sacred bark.

The most important scene in the sanctuary shows the king before the god Min, asking for the provision of many soldiers. Other scenes show the king before the bark of Amun-Re, offering perfume to the god Amun-Min, and the king before his own divine bark.

The architects and astronomers wrought magic in their design for this temple: twice each year, on February 22 and October 22, the rays of the sun come in through the front entrance and travel straight through the temple until they reach the inner sanctuary, where they illuminate the faces of the rock-cut statues of Amun, Re-Horakhti, and Ramesses II for a full twenty minutes. The face of Ptah, who is god of the underworld in one of his many guises, remains in darkness.

It has been suggested that this magical event represents the birth and ascension to the throne of Ramesses II, but I believe that this is only an astronomical feature.

Sanctuary of the Great Temple of Abu Simbel.

Other chapels

To the northeast of this temple is a chapel to the sun god, which was discovered by Barsanti when he was clearing the temple in 1910. A small part of this temple was cut into the rock, and the rest was built of quarried stone. On its eastern wall are two towers. Inside are two altars, to the left of which stood two statue groups. The first is of the god Thoth in the shape of a baboon, accompanied by a scarab beetle. The second shows four monkeys in attitudes of prayer and two small obelisks. These statue groups were taken to Aswan to be exhibited at the new Nubia Museum in Aswan. The walls of the chapel are decorated with religious scenes.

To the south of this chapel is another smaller chapel dedicated to Thoth. The walls of the outer hall were built of mudbrick; the sanctuary is cut into the rock. The religious scenes that decorated the walls of this sanctuary still retain traces of their beautiful original colors.

Clearly, Ramesses has represented himself among these gods to show his divinity. It would seem that the orientation of these chapels with the sun was designed to associate him with the sun god Re, so as a sequence in this association, Ramesses depicted himself as Re on the temple façade, as shown by the baboons rising to hail the sunrise.

The Temple
of Queen Nefertari

About 120 m (390 ft) to the north of the Great Temple lies the temple of Queen Nefertari (see plan page 81), which is also dedicated to Hathor. Like its larger companion, this temple is dug into the face and, though much smaller in size, it is still magnificent and very imposing. Inscribed on the façade of the temple is a text indicating that the builder (Ramesses II) is Ruler of Kush; it also states: I am from Herakleopolis.

The front of the temple is 28.3 m (93 ft) long and 12.2 m (40 ft) high. Six colossal statues grace the façade, three on each side of the entrance door. The two sides are the same: in the center is Queen Nefertari, flanked on either side by images of Ramesses II. The statues are 11.5 m (38 ft) high and each statue is accompanied by two small statues showing the children of the royal couple. On the left, King Ramesses II is shown with his two daughters Merit-Amun and Meri-Re. Nefertari is accompanied by Merit-Amun and Hanut-Tawir. The other statue of Ramesses is accompanied by the two princes Amen-hir-Khopshef and Rahirwenemef.

The façade of the Temple of Nefertari - Abu Simbel.

The two sides of the entrance (**1**) are carved with scenes of the king presenting wine to Re-Horakhti; the arches above the entrance are decorated with cartouches and texts about the king and queen.

From the entrance, a passage (**2**) leads to a square hall (**3**) whose ceiling rests on six square columns, each of which is surmounted by a head of Hathor. The images on the columns show the king and queen presenting offerings to different gods and goddesses.

The ceiling of this hall is carved with a text in which Ramesses II dedicates the temple to Queen Nefertari. The queen in Ancient Egypt was the embodiment of the goddess Hathor, who was the eye of the god Re, wife of the living king and mother of the future king.

Among the scenes in this hall we see the king, accompanied by the queen, as he is about to kill a Nubian prisoner before Amun-Re; the king before the goddess Hathor, and Ramesses II advancing towards the god Ptah in his palace. We also see Queen Nefertari before the goddess Hathor and King Ramesses offering wine to Re-Horakhti.

The pillared hall has three doors at the back all leading to a broad vestibule (**4**). The middle door is decorated with titles of Ramesses II. The vestibule itself is decorated with scenes of the king presenting wine to Re-Horakhti while the queen offers flowers to Khnum, Satet, and Anhket. In another scene the king presents flowers to Horus-Min, Horus-Baki, and Horus-Bohan, and wine to Amun-Re.

In the center of the west wall of this hall is a door leading to the inner sanctuary (**5**). This door is decorated with cartouches of the queen protected by the wings of the vulture goddess, Nekhbet.

In the western wall of the sanctuary is a niche containing a rock-cut statue of the goddess Hathor in the shape of a cow protecting King Ramesses.

The Square Hall of the Temple of Nefertari - Abu Simbel.

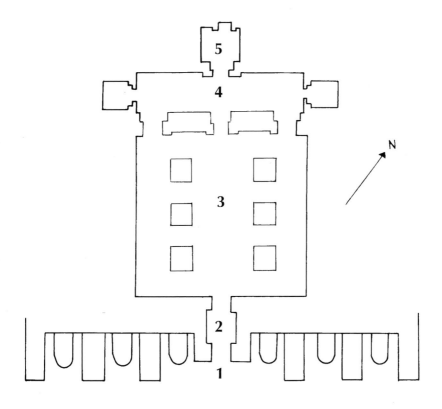

Plan of the Temple of Nefertari

Nineteenth-century drawing
of the two temples of Abu Simbel.

The Temples of Ramesses in Nubia

The great king Ramesses, known as the master of builders in ancient Egypt, built four temples in Nubia. After his time, for about one thousand years, no temples or chapels were built in Nubia.

The Temple of Beit el-Wali

This temple is located a short distance to the northwest of the temple of Kalabsha, about 55 km (34 miles) south of Aswan. It is cut in the rock and built on the surface of a mound. It is considered to be the oldest temple of Ramesses' reign. The temple is dedicated to the gods Khnum, Amun, and Anukis. During the Christian period, it was used as a church. During the Nubian salvage campaign, the temple was moved to the northwest of Kalabsha. It contains important scenes of the king's campaign against the Nubians.

The Temple of el-Sebua

The site of el-Sebua, located about 150 km (94 miles) south of Aswan, is the second largest temple in Nubia; it was originally built under the supervision of Setau, Ramesses' viceroy in Kush during years 35-50 of his reign. The site is known by this name for the lion-bodied sphinxes in front of the temple that in Arabic are often called *subu'* ("predatory animals, lions").

The temple is dedicated to the gods Amun, Re-Horakhti, and Ramesses himself. It is built of stone. The temple was moved in the years 1961–65 of salvage campaign and rebuilt on a site known as New el-Sebua, about 4 km (2.5 miles) west of the old site.

One of the sphinxes of the temple of el-Sebua.

The Temple of el-Derr

The Derr temple is located about 208 km (130 miles) south of Aswan. Dedicated to the gods Ptah of Memphis, Amun of Thebes, and Ramesses himself, it was cut in the rock during years 35–50 of Ramesses' reign. The temple walls contain scenes of Ramesses' campaign in Nubia.

It is the only temple in Nubia that was located on the eastern side of Lake Nasser. The temple was moved about 11 km (7 miles) southwest of the old site.

The Temple of el-Derr.

The Temple of Garf Hussein

Garf Hussein is a small temple built by Ramesses that is now in a poor state of preservation. Many additions were made to the temple during the Meroitic period. A large statue of Ramesses II that was here has been moved to the Nubian Museum. The original is now underwater; the temple itself was moved during the salvage campaign a little distance onto the shore.

Bibliography

Adams, W. Y. *Nubia, Corridor to Africa.* London: Allen Lane, 1977.

Baines, J. and J. Málek. *Atlas of Ancient Egypt.* Oxford: Phaidon, 1980.

Bernal, M. *Black Athena: The Afrocentric Roots of Classical Civilization.* New Brunswick, NJ: Rutgers University Press, 1987.

Butzer, K. W. and C. L. Hansen. *Desert and River in Nubia.* Madison, WI: University of Wisconsin Press, 1968.

Christophe, L.-A. *Abou Simbel et l'épopée de sa découverte.* Bruxelles: Merckx 1965.

Curto, S. *Nubia: Storia di una civilta favolosa.* Novara: Istituto Geograpfico de Agostini, 1965.

Davies, W. V., (ed.). *Egypt and Africa*: Nubia from Prehistory to Islam. London: British Museum Press in association with the Egypt Exploration Society, 1991.

Desroches-Noblecourt, Ch. and Ch. Kuentz. *Le petit temple d'Abou Simbel. I.* Cairo: Centre de documentation et d'étude sur l'ancienne Égypte, 1968.

Dunham, D. *The Royal Cemeteries of Kush.* Boston: Museum of Fine Arts and Harvard University Press, 1950–63.

_____. *The Barkal Temples.* Boston: Museum of Fine Arts, 1970.

Edwards, D. N. *Archaeology and Settlement in Upper Nubia in the First Millennium A.D.* Cambridge Monographs in African Archaeology 36, BAR International Series 537, 1989.

Firth, C. M. *The Archaeological Survey of Nubia, Report for 1901–1911.* Cairo: National Printing Dept., Maslahat al-Masahah, 1927.

Gohary, J. *Guide to the Nubian Monuments on Lake Nasser.* Cairo: The American University in Cairo Press, 1998.

Hinkel, F. W. *Exodus from Nubia.* Berlin: Akademie-Verlag, 1978.

Hawass, Z. *Silent Images: Women in Pharaonic Egypt.* Cairo: The American University in Cairo Press, 2000.

Hochfield, S. and E. Riefstahl (eds.). *Africa in Antiquity: The Arts of Ancient Nubia and the Sudan, Part 1: The Essays.* New York: Brooklyn Museum, 1978.

Kemp, B. J. *Ancient Egypt: Anatomy of a Civilization.* New York: Routledge, 1989.

Kitchen, K. A. *Pharaoh Triumphant: The Life and Time of Ramses II.* Cairo: The American University in Cairo Press, 1990.

Lichtheim, C. M. *Ancient Egyptian Literature, Vol. I: The Old and Middle Kingdoms.* Berkeley: The University of California Press, 1973.

Marks, A.E. *Preceramic Sites* (The Scandinavian Joint Expedition to Sudanese Nubia, Vol. 2). Stockholm: Munksgaard, 1970.

Nordström, H. A. *Neolithic and A-Group Sites* (The Scandinavian Joint Expedition to Sudanese Nubia, Vol. 3). Uppsala: Munksgaard, 1972.

O'Connor, D. *Ancient Nubia: Egypt's Rival in Africa.* Philadelphia: University of Pennsylvania, 1993.

Porter, B. and R. Moss. *Topographical Bibliography of Ancient Egyptian Texts, Reliefs, and Paintings. VII: Nubia, the Deserts, and Outside Egypt* (revised J. Málek, Griffith Institute). Oxford: Oxford University Press, 1995.

Reisner, G. A. T*he Archaeological Survey of Nubia, Report for 1907–1908, Vol. 1.* Cairo: Maslahat al-Masahah, 1910.

_____. *Excavations at Kerma.* Cambridge, MA: Peabody Museum of Harvard University, 1923.

Sadr, K. *The Development of Nomadism in Ancient Northeast Africa.* Philadelphia: University of Pennsylvania, 1991.

Säve-Söderbergh, T. *Temples and Tombs of Ancient Nubia: The International Rescue Campaign at Abu Simbel, Philae, and Other Sites.* New York: Thames & Hudson, 1987.

Shinnie, P. L. *Ancient Nubia.* New York: Kegan Paul International, 1996.

Siliotti, A. *Egypt: Temples, Men, and Gods.* Cairo: The American University in Cairo Press, 2001.

Taylor, J. *Egypt and Nubia.* Cambridge, MA: Harvard University Press, 1991.

Trigger, B. G. *Nubia under the Pharaohs.* London: Thames & Hudson, 1976.

Trigger, B. G., et al. *Ancient Egypt: A Social History.* New York: Cambridge University Press, 1994.

Vandier, J. *Manuel d'archéologie égyptienne.* Paris: Picard, 1952–58.

Weeks, K. *The Lost Tomb.* Cairo: The American University in Cairo Press, 1998.

Welsby, D. A. T*he Kingdom of Kush.* London: British Museum Press, 1996.

Wenig, S. T. "Nubien," in W. Helck and W. E. Otto (eds.), *Lexikon der Ägyptologie,* Band IV. Wiesbaden: Harrassowitz, 1980.

Wildung, D. (ed.). *Sudan: Ancient Kingdoms of the Nile.* New York: Flammarion 1997.

Williams, B. B. *The A-Group Royal Cemetery at Qustul (Excavations between Abu Simbel and the Sudan Frontier, Part 1).* Chicago: Oriental Institute of the University of Chicago, 1986.

Zaba, Z. *The Rock Inscriptions of Lower Nubia.* Prague: Charles University, 1974.